A SPECIAL DAY ON THE FARM

MELANIE RAE DAVIS

Copyright © 2024

All Rights Reserved

DEDICATION

"TO MY CHILDREN AND GRANDCHILDREN"

For every bedtime story whispered under starry skies, for the brave explorers who turn every page into an adventure, this book is dedicated to YOU.

May it be the bridge between generations, connecting the wonder of childhood to the wisdom of adulthood. Also, I hope you find joy, imagination, adventure and love within these pages..

With all my heart, Melanie.

ACKNOWLEDGMENT

"FOR MY CHILDREN AND GRANDCHILDREN"

To my children and grandchildren, you are the stars that light up my universe. May this book be a small gift in return for the happiness you bring to my life.

Also, to my Mother who inspired me to write this book.

ABOUT THE AUTHOR

Melanie is a first time children's book author with a passion for storytelling. She believes every child should be able to open their imagination and hopes her books inspire young readers to explore magical worlds, like A Special Day on The Farm! When she is not writing, Melanie loves taking long walks, horseback riding and bicycling, etc. Melanie believes, "If you have a dream in your heart, make it come true!"

STORY

Ellie, Billy, and their friendly cow, Betsy, live on a beautiful farm. There are green fields as far as the eye can see and a big red barn where the animals live. The farmhouse has a cozy kitchen where they eat breakfast together every morning. Betsy loves grazing in the sunny pasture, and Ellie and Billy love exploring the farm and playing in the tall grass. It's their special place where they spend happy days together, surrounded by nature's beauty.

Ellie and Billy share a special bond as brother and sister, united by their love for their farm and its animals. Their parents, always nearby, guide them with gentle hands and warm smiles. Together, they work as a team, feeding the chickens, grooming the horses, caring for Betsy, and playing in the fields. Laughter fills the air as they chase each other around the barnyard, their hearts full of joy and love for one another. In this close-knit family, every moment is cherished, and every day is an adventure.

As the sun rises over the farm, the air is filled with the sounds of nature - birds chirping, cows mooing, and the gentle rustle of leaves in the breeze. A new day begins filled with the charm of rural routines. Ellie and Billy eagerly prepare for their day ahead, knowing there are animals to feed, eggs to collect, and fields to explore. With a sense of excitement and anticipation, they set off on their daily adventures, ready to embrace the beauty and simplicity of farm life.

Ellie and Billy begin their day with the comforting routine of feeding Betsy and caring for Rosie the horse, Clucky the chicken, Gus the goose, and Percy the pig, ensuring each one is

well-fed and happy. With sleepy smiles and hearts full of love, they greet each animal with tender care, knowing that they are part of a special family. The soft sounds of hooves and chirping birds fill the air as they work together in harmony, surrounded by the peaceful beauty of the countryside. In this quiet moment, amidst the golden glow of morning, they feel a deep sense of belonging and happiness.

As the morning sun casts its golden glow, Ellie and Billy share tender moments with their beloved cow, Betsy. With gentle strokes, they brush her soft coat, feeling her warmth beneath their touch. While Betsy responds with soft nudges, they also tend to Rosie the horse, Clucky the chicken, Gus the goose, Percy the pig, Daisy the duck, and Gary the goat. Together, they work in harmony, dividing tasks with practiced ease, while all the animals follow them closely, their presence a source of comfort and joy. In the quiet of the farm awakening, their bond grows stronger, showing their love and friendship.

On the farm, Ellie, Billy, Betsy, Mom, and Dad are all one big happy family. They work together like a team, with everyone having a special job to do. Mom and Dad help Ellie and Billy take care of Betsy, showing them the ropes and making sure everything runs smoothly. In return, Betsy provides them all with delicious milk and lots of love! They also have Charlie the cat, Max the dog, Sammy the sheep, and Ruby the rabbit as part of their loving farm family. Together, they create a warm and joyful atmosphere where everyone is cherished and cared for.

Together, they laugh and play, turning chores into fun adventures. Whether it's feeding the animals or raking out the barn, they do it with smiles on their faces and love in their hearts. On their farm, family is everything, and they wouldn't have it any other way.

With everyone working together, they know that by sharing their responsibilities, they make their farm a happy and thriving place to be. And as they work side by side, they strengthen their bond as a family, making every day on the farm an adventure filled with love and laughter.

Betsy, the friendly cow on the farm, has a personality as big as her heart. With her adorable brown eyes and playful antics, she brings endless joy and excitement to Ellie and Billy's daily routine. Whether she's munching on hay with gusto or giving them gentle nudges as they work, Betsy's mischievous spirit adds a touch of fun to their chores. But amidst all her playful antics, Betsy's presence is a source of comfort and happiness for Ellie and Billy, making their farm life even more special.

As days turn into weeks on the farm, Betsy's playful nature makes her feel like another member of the family. Laughter fills the air as Ellie, Billy, Mom, and Dad share in her playful behavior. Whether she's stealing a nibble of hay or giving gentle nudges as they work, Betsy's presence adds joy and spontaneity to their daily routine. Their farm feels complete with her around, bringing everyone closer together with her lovable personality.

One sunny day, while exploring the farm, Ellie and Billy stumble upon a secret meadow hidden behind a row of tall trees. As they venture deeper into the meadow, they find delightful surprises at every turn. Colorful flowers sway in the gentle breeze while butterflies dance around. In the center of the meadow, a little stream flows peacefully, inviting them to splash in its clear waters. Their ordinary farm exploration turns into an exciting adventure, full of wonder and joy at the treasures they discover.

During their daily chores, Ellie and Billy stumble upon unexpected treasures that fill their hearts with wonder. As they journey through the farm, they discover a hidden spot bathed in sunlight, perfect for a wholesome picnic. With Mom and Dad by their side, they spread out a cozy blanket and unpack a delicious lunch prepared by Mom. With the gentle breeze whispering through the trees and the birds singing overhead, they enjoy each bite, surrounded by nature's beauty. It's a magical moment where simple pleasures and unexpected discoveries come together to create lasting memories for the whole family.

After finding the sunny spot, Ellie and Billy help Mom and Dad unpack yummy food from the farm. They marvel at the colorful fruits and vegetables, knowing they were grown right on their farm. With big smiles and hungry tummies, they eat a tasty meal together. As they enjoy the good food and time with family, they remember how special it is to work together and enjoy what they've grown. It's a happy time full of love and the yummy things from their farm.

After their satisfying meal, Ellie and Billy approach their chores with imagination and creativity. They turn feeding the chickens into a race, seeing who can fill the feeders the fastest. Meanwhile, they enjoy grooming Sparky the horse, brushing his mane and tail until they shine in the sunlight. With laughter and fun, they turn their chores into games, making them more enjoyable than ever before.

With their chores done and their hearts full of happiness, they gather with Mom, Dad, and Betsy for a hearty dinner made from the bounty of their farm. The table is filled with delicious dishes made from fresh vegetables, eggs, and milk—all grown and produced right on their farm. With laughter and conversation flowing freely, they share stories of their day and express gratitude for the blessings of farm life. It's a time of togetherness and happiness, where the simple pleasures of family and food bring warmth to their hearts.

After their hearty dinner, Ellie, Billy, Mom, and Dad gather around the fire to share stories and reflections on the day's adventures. They talk about the fun they had exploring the farm, the games they played, and the delicious food they enjoyed together. As they chat and laugh, they feel grateful for the blessings of farm life and the love of their family. With the sun setting in the distance and a cool breeze coming in, they step outside to enjoy the peaceful evening scene.

As the night falls, the farm becomes quiet and peaceful, with twinkling stars filling the sky like tiny sparkling diamonds. Ellie, Billy, Mom, and Dad step outside and gaze up at the glittering canopy above them. They feel a sense of contentment and togetherness, surrounded by the beauty of nature and the love of their family. With a gentle breeze brushing against their cheeks, they know that they are exactly where they belong. As they head inside, ready for a cozy night's sleep, they carry with them the warm and reassuring feeling of familial love and the magic found in a day on the farm.